BOOZHOO, AJIDAMOO
by
Michael Lyons

©2014

Tribal Library
Saginaw Chippewa Indian Tribe
7070 E. Broadway
Mt. Pleasant MI 48858

WITHDRAWN

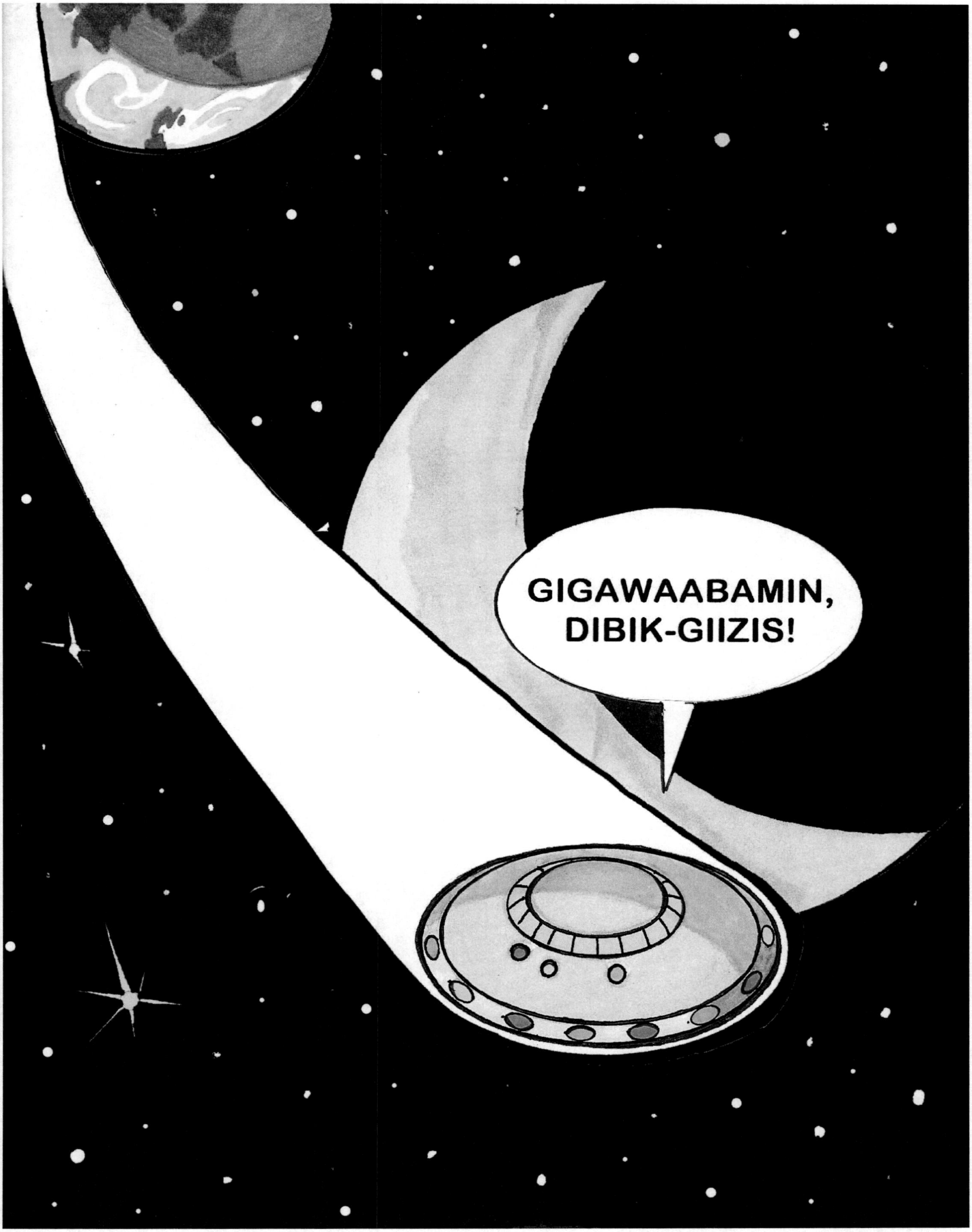
GIGAWAABAMIN, DIBIK-GIIZIS!

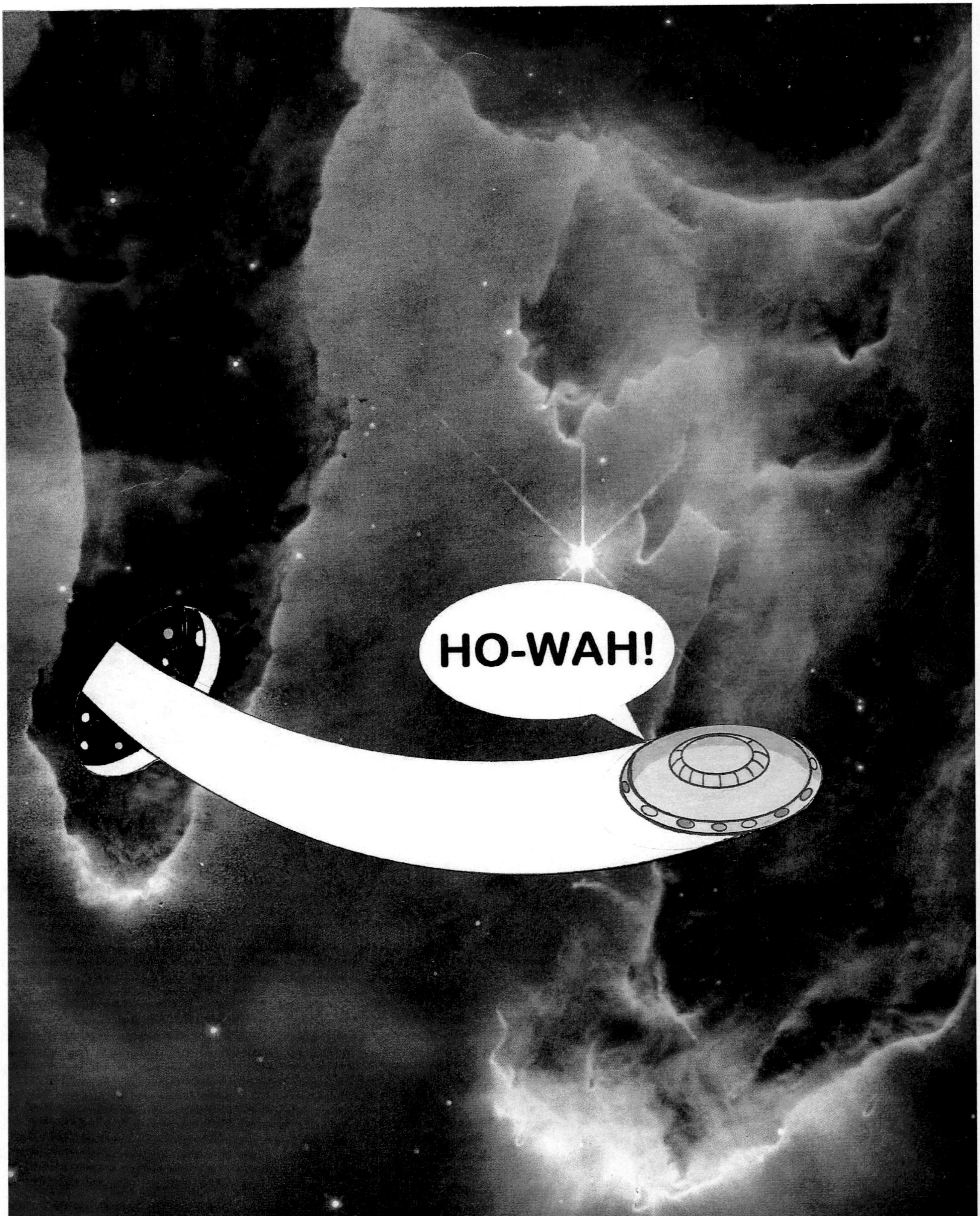
HO-WAH!

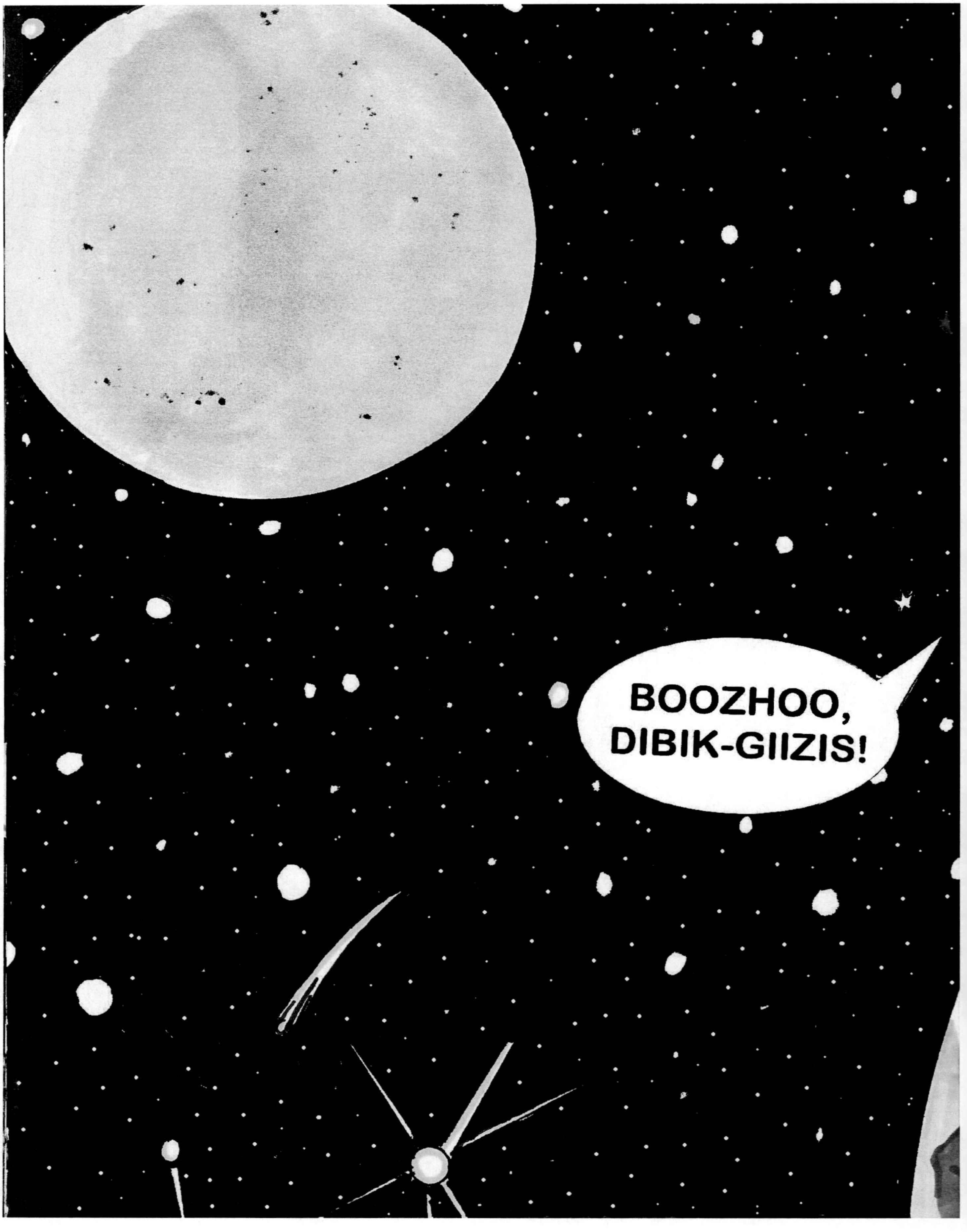
BOOZHOO, DIBIK-GIIZIS!

Other books by Michael Lyons available on Amazon.com:

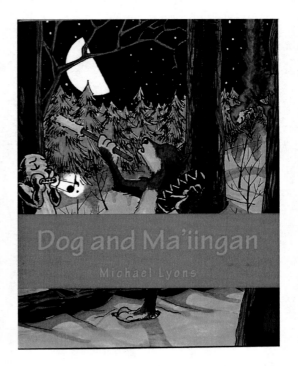

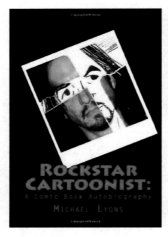

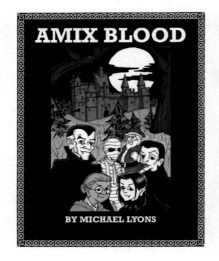

Contact Michael Lyons at: mlyons1984@yahoo.com

23337223R00021

Made in the USA
Middletown, DE
22 August 2015